ALFRED's

SACRED PERFORMER

DUETS

GO, TELL IT ON THE M...

Distinctive Duet Arrangements for Advent and Christmas

Arranged by *Victor Labenske*

"The virgin will be with Child and will give birth to a Son… For unto us a Child is born… A shoot will come up from the stump of Jesse; from his roots a Branch will bear fruit…" (Isaiah 7:14, 9:6, 11:1)

From the beautiful paraphrase of these scriptures in *Lo, How a Rose E'er Blooming,* to Luke's account of the angelic appearance to the shepherds in *Hark! The Herald Angels Sing*, the six carols included in this collection tell the good news of Jesus' birth, and anticipate the great sacrifice He made so that we might find salvation through Him. No wonder we celebrate the good news of Christmas.

Performing music with a duet partner is such a wonderful experience. I'm sure you will enjoy sharing these four-hand arrangements of some of the best-loved carols in your Christmas performances for years to come. In each performance, I hope you will think about the great words of these carols, and that through your music you will "Go, tell it on the mountain, that Jesus Christ is born!"

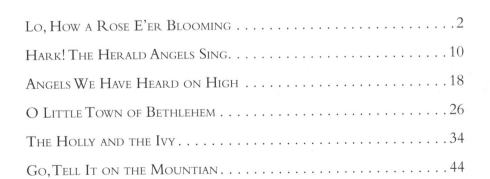

Alfred

Lo, How a Rose E'er Blooming

SECONDO

Michael Praetorius
Arr. Victor Labenske

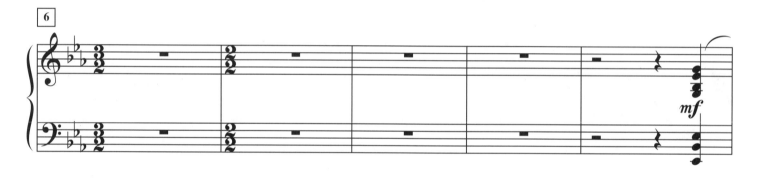

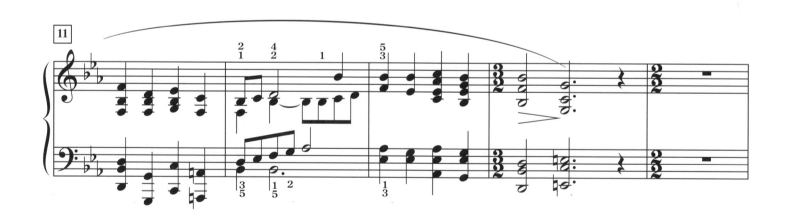

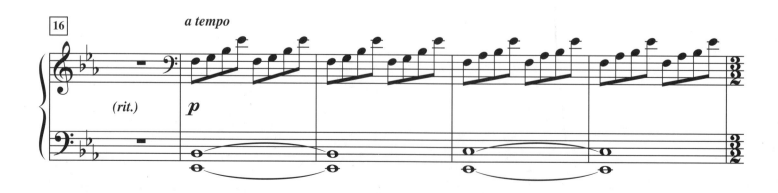

Lo, How a Rose E'er Blooming

PRIMO

Michael Praetorius
Arr. Victor Labenske

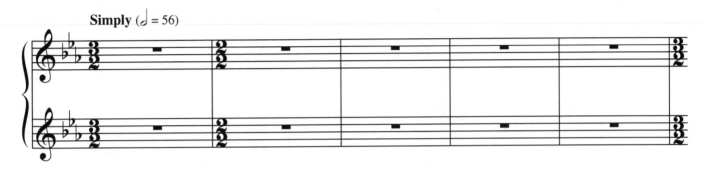

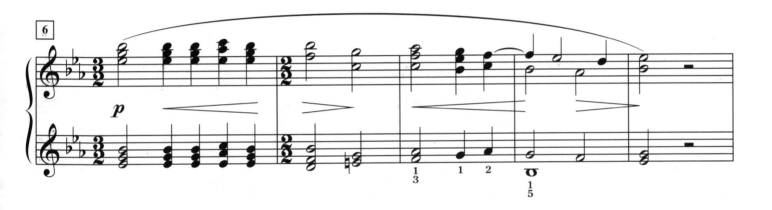

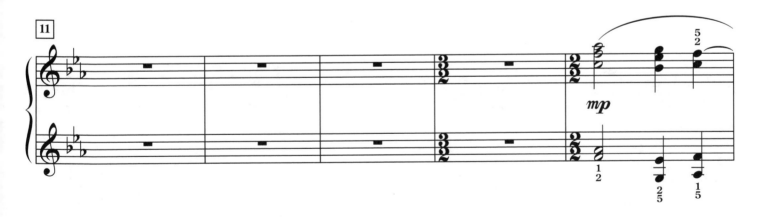

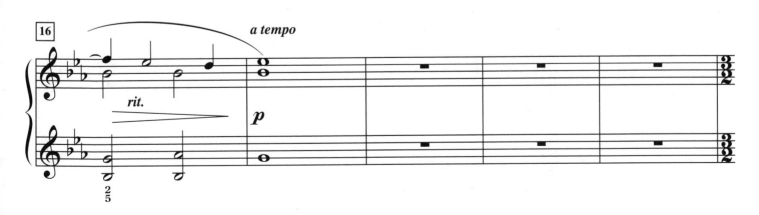

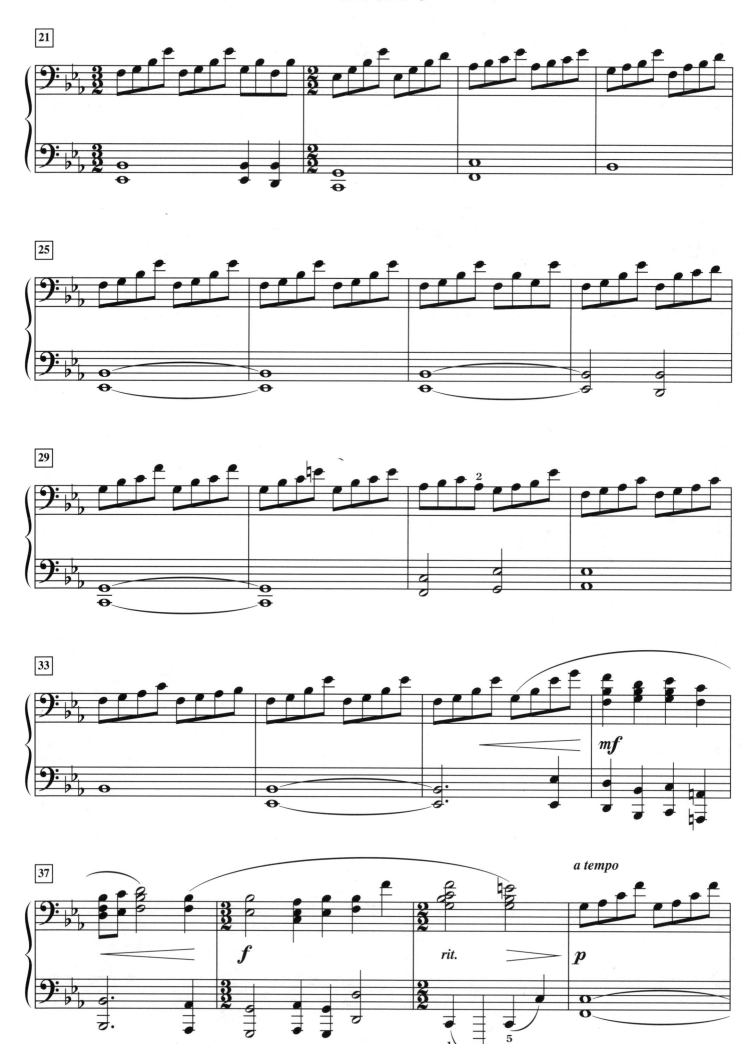

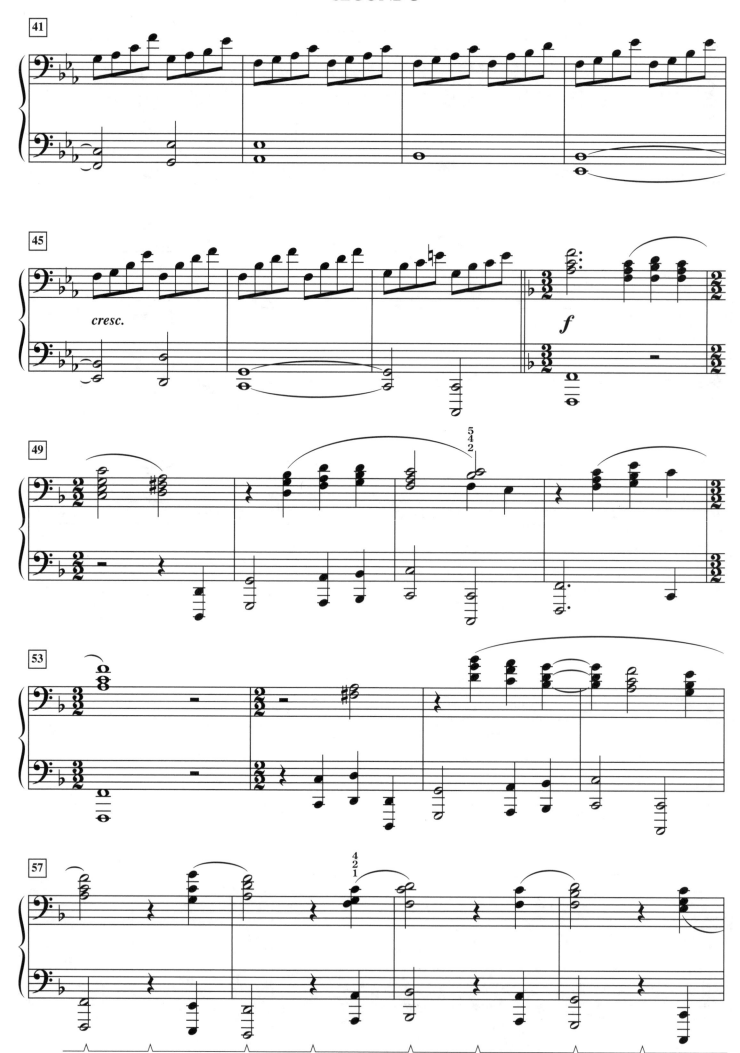

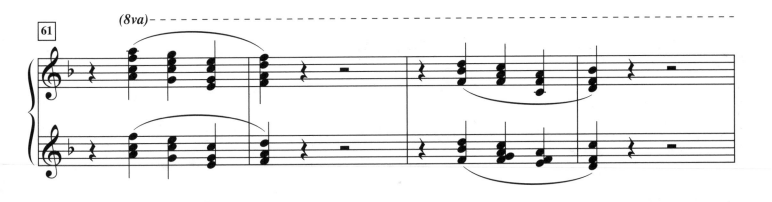

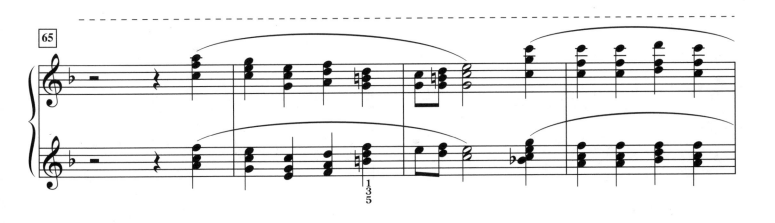

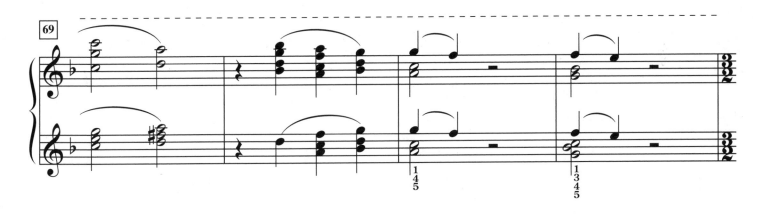

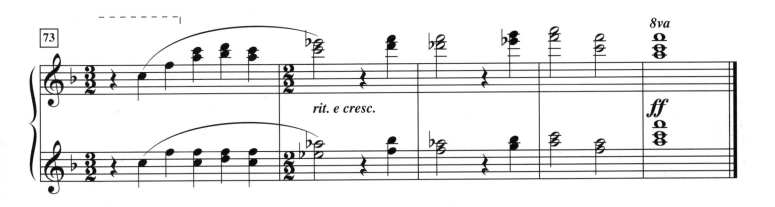

HARK! THE HERALD ANGELS SING

SECONDO

Felix Mendelssohn
Arr. Victor Labenske

Hark! The Herald Angels Sing

PRIMO

Felix Mendelssohn
Arr. Victor Labenske

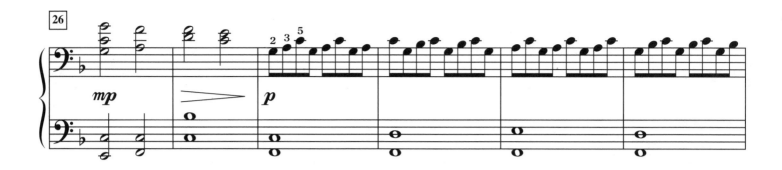

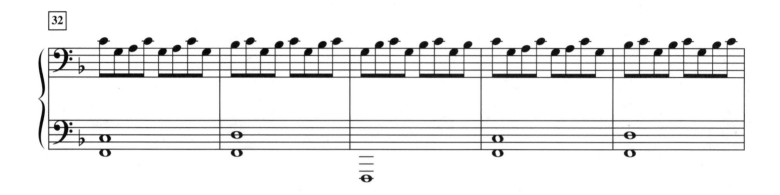

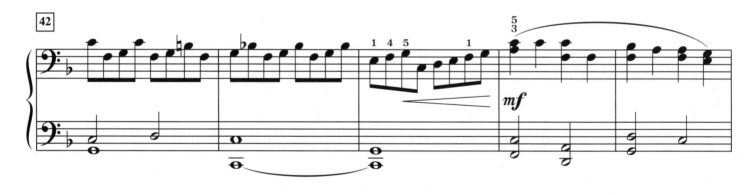

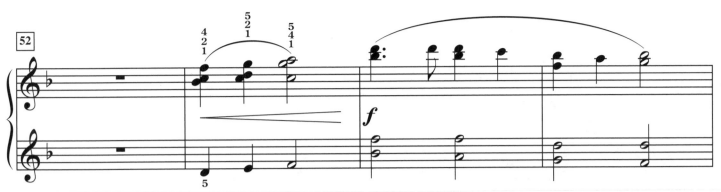

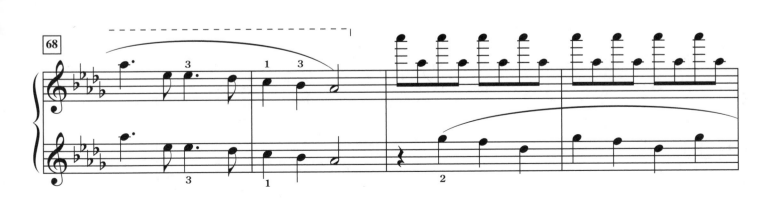

Angels We Have Heard On High

SECONDO

Traditional
Arr. Victor Labenske

ANGELS WE HAVE HEARD ON HIGH

PRIMO

Traditional
Arr. Victor Labenske

Calypso feel (♩. = 120)

(♪ = ♪ throughout)

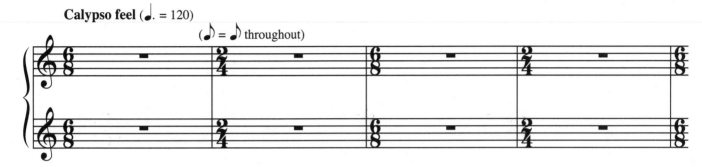

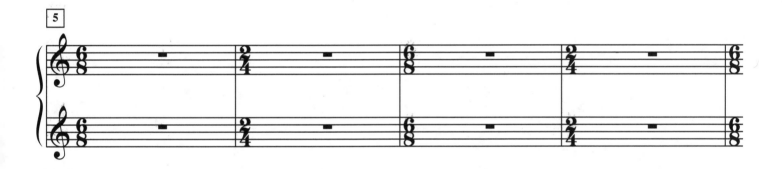

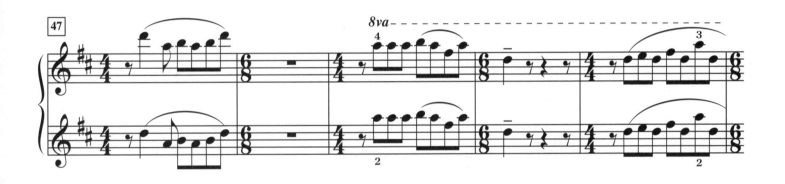

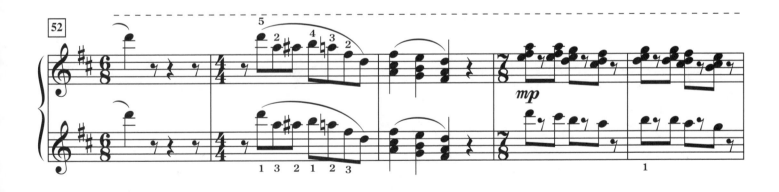

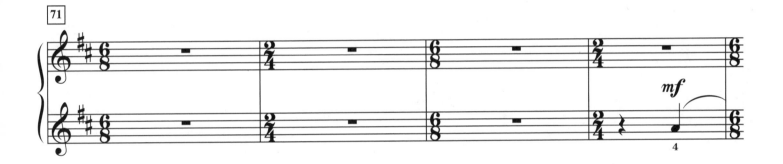

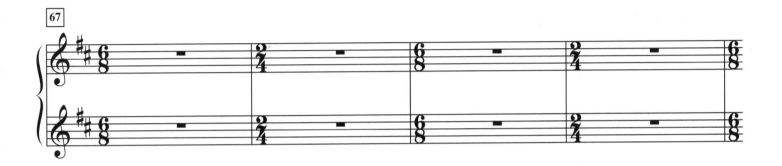

O Little Town of Bethlehem

SECONDO

Lewis H. Redner
Arr. Victor Labenske

O LITTLE TOWN OF BETHLEHEM

PRIMO

Lewis H. Redner
Arr. Victor Labenske

SECONDO

(pedal ad lib.)

THE HOLLY AND THE IVY

SECONDO

Traditional
Arr. Victor Labenske

THE HOLLY AND THE IVY

PRIMO

Traditional
Arr. Victor Labenske

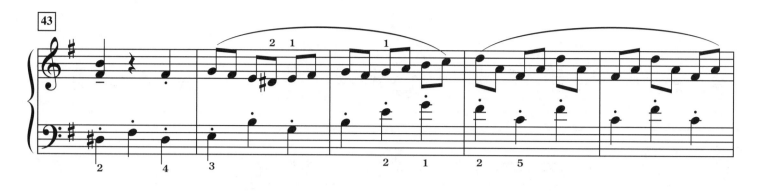

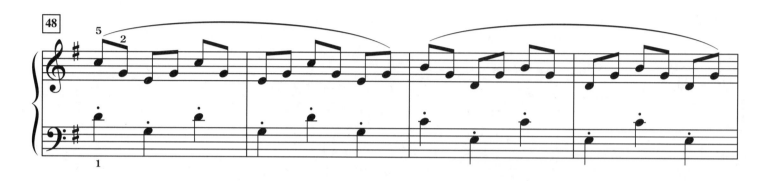

Go, Tell It on the Mountain

SECONDO

Spiritual
Arr. Victor Labenske

GO, TELL IT ON THE MOUNTAIN

PRIMO

Spiritual
Arr. Victor Labenske

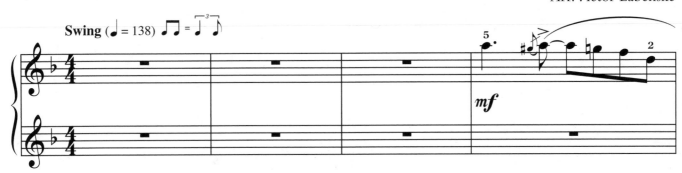

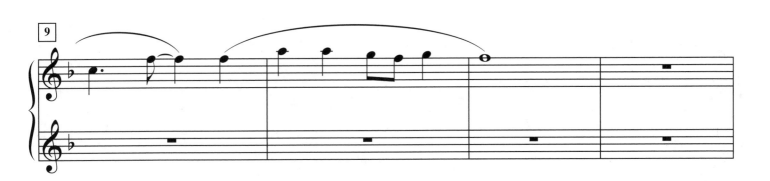

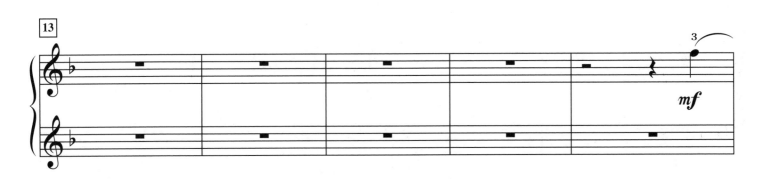

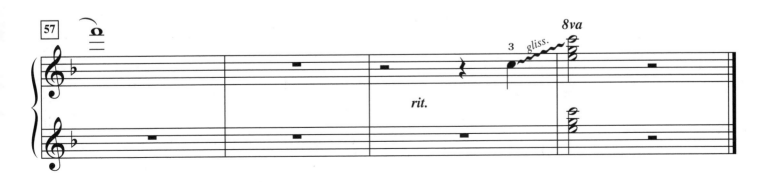

Lo, How a Rose E'er Blooming

Words: 15th-century German carol
(Verses 1-2 translated by Theodore Baker
Verse 3 by Friedrich Layritz, translated by Harriet K. Spaeth)
Music: Michael Praetorius

Lo, how a Rose e'er blooming from tender stem hath sprung!
Of Jesse's lineage coming, as those of old have sung.
It came, a floweret bright, amid the cold of winter,
When half-spent was the night.

Isaiah 'twas foretold it, the Rose I have in mind;
With Mary we behold it, the virgin mother kind.
To show God's love aright, she bore to us a Savior,
When half-spent was the night.

The shepherds heard the story proclaimed by angels bright,
How Christ, the Lord of glory was born on earth this night.
To Bethlehem they sped and in the manger they found Him,
As angel heralds said.

Hark! The Herald Angels Sing

Words: Charles Wesley
Music: Felix Mendelssohn

Hark! The herald angels sing,
"Glory to the newborn King!
Peace on earth, and mercy mild,
God and sinners reconciled."
Joyful, all ye nations, rise;
Join the triumph of the skies.
With th'angelic host proclaim,
"Christ is born in Bethlehem."
Hark! The herald angels sing,
"Glory to the newborn King!"

Christ, by highest heav'n adored!
Christ, the everlasting Lord!
Long desired, behold Him come,
Offspring of the Virgin's womb.
Veiled in flesh the Godhead see;
Hail th'incarnate Deity,
Pleased as man with men to dwell,
Jesus, our Emmanuel!
Hark! The herald angels sing,
"Glory to the newborn King!"

Hail, the heav'n born Prince of Peace!
Hail, the Sun of Righteousness!
Light and life to all He brings,
Ris'n with healing in His wings.
Mild He lays His glory by,
Born that man no more may die,
Born to raise the sons of earth,
Born to give them second birth.
Hark! The herald angels sing,
"Glory to the newborn King!"

Angels We Have Heard on High
Traditional French Carol

Angels we have heard on high,
Sweetly singing o'er the plains,
And the mountains in reply,
Echoing their joyous strains.

Come to Bethlehem, and see
Him whose birth the angels sing;
Come, adore on bended knee
Christ the Lord, the newborn King.

Refrain:
Gloria in excelsis Deo!
Gloria in excelsis Deo!

O Little Town of Bethlehem
Words: Phillips Brooks
Music: Lewis H. Redner

O little town of Bethlehem,
How still we see thee lie!
Above thy deep and dreamless sleep
The silent stars go by.
Yet in thy dark streets shineth
The everlasting Light;
The hopes and fears of all the years
Are met in thee tonight.

For Christ is born of Mary;
And gathered all above,
While mortals sleep, the angels keep
Their watch of wondering love.
O morning stars, together
Proclaim the holy birth;
And praises sing to God, the King,
And peace to men on earth.

O holy Child of Bethlehem,
Descend on us, we pray.
Cast out our sin, and enter in;
Be born in us today.
We hear the Christmas angels
The great glad tidings tell.
O come to us; abide with us,
Our Lord Emmanuel.

The Holly and the Ivy
Traditional

The holly and the ivy
Now both are full well grown,
Of all the trees that are in the wood
The holly bears the crown.

The holly bears a blossom
As white as lily flow'r,
And Mary bore sweet Jesus Christ
To be our sweet Savior.

The holly bears a berry
As red as any blood,
And Mary bore sweet Jesus Christ
To do poor sinners good.

Refrain:
O the rising of the sun,
The running of the deer,
The playing of the merry organ,
Sweet singing in the choir.

Go, Tell It on the Mountain
Words: John W. Work, Jr.
Music: Spiritual

Refrain:
Go, tell it on the mountain,
Over the hills and everywhere;
Go, tell it on the mountain
That Jesus Christ is born!

While shepherds kept their watching
O'er silent flocks by night,
Behold! Throughout the heavens
There shone a holy light.

The shepherds feared and trembled
When lo! Above the earth
Rang out the angel chorus
That hailed our Savior's birth.